SAKHUMZIJUB
ASE

HOW TO DEFEAT JUSTICE PART (I)

How to Defeat Justice

Jubase sakhumzi

Published by Jubase sakhumzi, 2022.

HOW TO DEFEAT JUSTICE

First edition. May 10, 2022.

ISBN: 979-8231579242

Written by Jubase sakhumzi.

Also by Jubase sakhumzi

How to Defeat Justice

Watch for more at https://sakhumzijubase.co.za.

To the defenders of truth and the keepers of hope, may your persistence remind the world that justice cannot be permanently defeated.

"The measure of a society is not found in its laws, but in how faithfully it upholds them when power tempts it to do otherwise."

How to defeat justice part(I): ***Journey through stigma, silence and survival***

Editing : Sakhumzi Jubase
Cover design: Sakhumzi Jubase
Illustrations: Sakhumzi Jubase
Phone: (+27) 87 5100 333
(+27) 60 393 2542

Edited in South Africa

Published by: Sakhumzi Jubase
Strachan street
Gauteng
Germiston-1401

Table of Contents

MAIN CHAPTERS

Foreword

This book is written in simple, direct language, drawn from independent personal experience and firsthand knowledge of how the very rules meant to protect justice can be broken to defeat it.

Its purpose is to raise awareness of crimes committed against civilians particularly by public officials acting in collaboration with street-level criminals. Through this account, I seek to warn readers how the arm of justice can be manipulated, leading innocent people to be arrested, prosecuted, and even imprisoned for crimes they never committed.

Some victims are forced to surrender their valuables under threat of prosecution or detention, pressured through false claims and extortion.

I share my own experience of being hijacked by a group of criminals, only to be later arrested and prosecuted on fabricated allegations. My vehicle, the very object of that crime, was seized by the same officials who should have protected me.

The perpetrators used lifelike toy or doll and falsified documents including false witness statements to build a criminal case. During court proceedings, unauthenticated documents authorized by officials from various departments were accepted without verification.

This book is dedicated to every South African and every person around the world, who has faced injustice, been silenced or stood alone against corruption. May these pages remind you that your voice matters, your truth is powerful and your courage is never wasted.

Together, across borders and backgrounds, we can expose wrongdoing, challenge abuse and build a more accountable and inclusive society for all.

Crime and corruption remain serious threats to our communities. This book exposes the fraudulent acts committed by street criminals in partnership with officials who, under the guise of public service, abuse their authority to defeat justice and harm the uninformed, poor, defenseless and innocent.

Author's Note

I hope you find this book positive and informative.

My name is Sakhumzi Jubase. I was born and raised in South Africa. I am a former employee who chose to speak out. This book is not just a reflection of my personal experience; it is a warning to the public.

I wrote *How to Defeat Justice* to expose how innocent civilians can be targeted, silenced and harmed through false allegations and institutional abuse. My story is one of survival, but also of strategy, truth and resistance. I believe that by sharing it, others may find strength to challenge injustice wherever it hides. When a person is wrongfully accused, society rarely waits for the verdict.

After my arrest in 2018, the most painful punishment was not the cell, it was the distance that grew between me and the world I once knew. I had walked into the justice system believing that truth would speak for itself. I came out realizing that once a person is branded, truth becomes a voice people are afraid to hear.

I was no longer Sakhumzi the advisor, the friend, the son, or the professional. I had become a story, one told without my participation. Everywhere I went, I could feel it. The hesitant greetings. The half finished conversations. The polite avoidance.

People who had once sought my advice now crossed the street when they saw me coming. Even those who believed in me whispered their support behind closed doors, terrified of being associated with my name in public.

At first, I tried to understand. I told myself they were afraid, not of me, but of what standing beside me might cost them. But with each passing year, that understanding grew heavy. Seven years later, the silence still echoes.

Stigma does not only isolate, it erases. It steals identity piece by piece, work, community, belonging, purpose. I lost my career in finance, the independence I had worked for and even my sense of home. I had to rely on others just to survive, an unbearable burden for someone who had built life through self reliance.

There were days when I woke up feeling like a stranger in my own life. The routines I once followed with confidence became heavy with doubt. I questioned my worth, my sanity and whether the fight for truth was worth the loneliness it brought.

I tried journaling, walking, praying and anything to quiet the storm inside. But the hardest part wasn't the pain. It was the invisibility. The feeling that no one saw the injustice, that no one wanted to. I learned to carry my emotions like a second skin, not to suppress them, but to understand them.

Anger taught me where boundaries had been crossed. Sadness reminded me of what I valued. And hope, fragile as it was, kept me moving. In the silence, I turned inward. Faith became less about religion and more about resilience, the belief that something greater than injustice still existed.

I didn't always pray with words. Sometimes, just breathing was a prayer. Just standing up was a declaration. I found comfort in small things, a sunrise, a child's laughter, a stranger's kindness. These moments reminded me that the world still held beauty, even when it felt broken.

My faith was not in institutions. It was in conscience. In the quiet conviction that truth, even when buried, cannot be destroyed. I remember one afternoon in Germiston, walking past a group of former colleagues. They saw me. I saw them. But no one spoke. One of them turned away, pretending to check his phone. Another gave a nod, the kind that says "I see you, but I can't be seen with you."

Another time, I attended a community meeting about rights education. I had been invited. But when I arrived, the organizer pulled me aside and said, "We're grateful for your work, but some attendees are uncomfortable. Maybe it's best if you don't speak today."

I left quietly. Not because I agreed, but because I understood the fear. And I knew that my voice would find another room, another audience, another moment. When you are isolated long enough, you realize that dignity is not given by society, it is claimed by standing for what you know is right.

That realization became my turning point. I stopped trying to prove my worth to those who refused to see it, and started focusing on those who still needed a voice. Every time I stand before a small group, teaching them about rights, the rule of law, or how to prepare for court, I feel whole again.

Even if only a handful attend, I know that I am rebuilding something, not just my life, but the idea that no lie can permanently bury truth. The hardest truth I've learned is that stigma in South Africa is not just about individuals, it's a symptom of fear. People fear truth because truth demands accountability. They fear association because association might force them to act. But silence is not safety. It's complicity dressed as comfort.

Every time a community withdraws from a person in pain, it strengthens the hands of those who abuse power. Today, I still live with the weight of stigma. Opportunities are few. Support is scarce. Many remain hesitant. But I also live with something far greater, peace with my conscience and faith in my mission. Isolation may have taken away crowds, but it gave me clarity.

Stigma may have broken public trust, but it strengthened my inner one. And perhaps the most powerful realization of all is that, "You cannot be silenced by a world you no longer need to please." I continue to walk, even when alone, because if truth though delayed, it will always finds its way back to light.

Chapter 01
EXT nine formal settlement

Germiston is a city in the East Rand of Gauteng, South Africa and forms part of the Ekurhuleni Metropolitan Municipality. Extension 9 (EXT9), a modest but resilient township in the eastern region of Gauteng, South Africa. Nestled just 8 km from the Germiston central business district, EXT9 is part of the Ekurhuleni Metropolitan Municipality and sits at the corner of Simmons Backer Road and Lower Boksburg Road.

It's a place where tarred streets and electrified homes reflect both government investment and the quiet determination of families who've upgraded their RDP houses with pride and perseverance. Growing up in EXT9 meant living in a community of fewer than 30,000 households, surrounded by the hum of factories in Germiston South.

These industrial giants some of them multinational brands, provided employment to many locals. While formal businesses were scarce, the informal economy thrived. Spaza shops and hair salons dotted the streets, 99.8% of them owned by foreign nationals.

The remaining 0.2% local taverns and eateries offered traditional dishes like chicken dust, fish and chips, served with warmth and familiarity. Our community is 100% Black African, multilingual and culturally rich. Zulu, Xhosa, Sepedi, and other South African languages filled the air, alongside a few foreign tongues brought in by migrant entrepreneurs. Football was our heartbeat, especially among the youth but we had no formal playing fields.

Matches are held in neighboring locations and one open public gym stood as our only recreational facility. Education was a challenge. EXT9 had no schools of its own, only day-care centers for young children. The nearest primary school was in Extension 8, Dukathole. Public transport was our lifeline minibus taxis ferried workers and learners daily, though the absence of formal taxi ranks often led to congestion and safety risks.

Despite these limitations, EXT9 shaped me. It taught me resilience, resourcefulness and the power of community. I saw how people made the most of what they had, how they built homes, businesses and lives with limited means. I learned that development isn't just about infrastructure, it's about dignity, opportunity and inclusion.

Today, I carry EXT9 with me in everything I do. My work is rooted in the belief that communities like mine deserve more, more schools, more youth centers, more support for local entrepreneurs and safer, smarter transport systems. I advocate for formal business zones, microfinance for local ownership and recreational spaces that nurture talent and pride.

EXT9 is not just where I reside from, it's why I do what I do. It's the foundation of my leadership, my vision and my commitment to building a South Africa where every township is seen, heard and empowered.

Chapter 02

The hijacking of the car

It was payday, the last day of August 2018 and the following day marked the beginning of November. That morning, I spent a few hours at work, from 08:30 until 10:40. After leaving the office with a colleague, we traveled to Extension 9.

Later in the day, we returned to the city of Germiston with two individuals who had come into town for shopping. I spent part of the afternoon at an internet café and later relaxed at a nearby park. As evening approached, we decided to head back to Extension 9. We left around 19:40 and arrived by 20:00, following a short 10–15-minute drive.

We entered Extension 9 via Sezela Street, a residential road that connects directly to Mfula Street, the township's main thoroughfare. The house we were visiting was located just two houses away from Mfula Street, along Sezela Street. The area is fully electrified and streetlights provided clear visibility throughout the route.

As we neared our destination, driving at a cautious speed of approximately 15–20 km/h appropriate for a residential zone, we noticed two women standing on the left side of the road, facing our direction. From a distance of about 30 meters, we could see them clearly under the streetlights. As we approached, they began waving their hands to get our attention. In South Africa, finger pointing and hand waving are common, culturally recognized gestures used by pedestrians to signal for a lift whether from public transport or private vehicles.

On that evening, as we approached our destination in Extension 9, we noticed two women standing outside a house, just a few steps from the yard fence. They were using both gestures pointing and waving to get our attention. I wasn't alone in the car. The passengers insisted that we stop and hear what they had to say. Their house was located in a well-lit residential part of the neighborhood, not considered dangerous and it was just one house away from the place we were visiting.

In a small community like Extension 9, especially among women, people tend to know one another. That familiarity gave us a sense of safety and trust. We slowed down and stopped the car. The street was illuminated by functioning streetlights and we were driving at a cautious speed between 15 and 20 km/h, as is recommended in residential zones. We rolled down the left window to listen.

One of the women appeared visibly distressed. Her voice trembled and she seemed on the verge of tears. "Please," she pleaded, "help me take my child to the hospital. "Is injured. "Her desperation was unmistakable. In that moment, we saw not strangers, but community members in need.

We had no reason to suspect danger. We were close to our destination, surrounded by familiar streets and responding to what looked like a genuine cry for help. What followed would challenge everything we thought we knew about trust, justice and the hidden dangers that can lurk behind familiar faces and familiar places.

Chapter 03
The trap behind the plea

In a small community like Extension 9, neighbors know each other personally. When someone is attacked, the first people to hear their cries for help are often those living just a few steps away. In such a setting, ignoring a plea for assistance would be considered inhuman, especially when the call comes from someone familiar, someone trusted.

That night, the women who flagged us down were standing outside their home, just a few steps from the yard fence. Their house was next to the one we were visiting and they were known to the people we had come to see. As we approached, one of the passengers in my car urged us to stop and listen. The women appeared desperate and in a community like ours, especially among women, such gestures are taken seriously.

I got out of the car to hear them more clearly. One of the women, visibly distressed, pleaded, "Please help me take my child to the hospital. He's injured." Her voice trembled with urgency. They stood on the left edge of the road, facing our direction. Both women were Black Africans, likely between the ages of 25 and 40.

Concerned, I asked, "What happened to the child?" "Injured," she replied, her voice strained and emotional. I then asked, "Can I see the child?" What I was handed was not a child but a lifelike toy or doll. It was wet, dressed in a toddler's sleeping overall, dark in color, possibly black or navy, with bright or white star patterns. It was wrapped in a small blanket.

Because it was evening and the streetlights weren't close enough, I couldn't clearly distinguish the exact colors. The doll was cold and damp and I held it briefly against my chest before realizing something was wrong. "This is a toy," I said. "Where is the child?" Before I could get a response, the woman who handed me the doll snatched it back. The other woman grabbed me forcefully.

Suddenly, others emerged, people I hadn't seen before. I don't know where they had been hiding, but they joined in immediately. A group of women, possibly six to ten in number, along with young boys and children, surrounded me. Altogether, there were about eleven individuals, maybe more, but all appeared to be under fifteen in total.

They began to assault me. I was stripped of my shirt during the attack. I didn't stand passively. I tried to push them away, to defend myself but I was overwhelmed. Their assault was relentless and I couldn't escape. Eventually, a tall, dark-hefty man appeared. He wore white shorts and a white sleeveless top. He tried to intervene, but they ignored him. The attack continued. A few minutes later, I saw a white bakkie approaching, a Ford Ranger with a canopy.

Its arrival marked a turning point, but at the time, I didn't know whether it signaled help or something far worse. By the time the Ford Ranger arrived, both my colleague and my vehicle had already left the scene. The Ranger came to a halt across the street, blocking both lanes of traffic. Its size and position effectively divided the road, obscuring visibility for anyone traveling along Mfula Street, the main road in Extension 9.

From that moment, whatever was happening on the other side of the vehicle was hidden from view. The driver of the Ranger was a local resident and my former landlord, from whom I had previously rented a parking space. Upon arrival, he stepped out of the vehicle and confronted the group that had gathered, firmly instructing them to stop their aggressive behavior. Remarkably, they complied without resistance or physical intervention.

At that point, another man, who had been attempting to intervene earlier led me to the back of the Ranger and locked me inside the canopy. From within, I could hear voices shouting threats, "If the child dies, we will kill you." I was overwhelmed with confusion and fear. I had no knowledge of any child or what they were referring to, yet the threats were direct and chilling.

Terrified and uncertain of what might happen next, I decided not to wait passively. I searched for a way out and managed to open a small window in the canopy. With great effort, I squeezed through the opening and escaped. At that moment, I was stripped of my upper clothing, barefoot, without a belt, wearing only trousers. My legs were in pain, so I couldn't run. I crawled slowly toward Mfula Street, staying low. The crowd had gathered on the right side of the vehicle, while I exited from the left.

The Ranger remained parked across the road and I wasn't sure if anyone had seen me. Fortunately, I was able to slip away without being chased. I continued crawling until I reached the main road and crossed it, seeking refuge in an open, unlit area beyond. The darkness provided cover and I remained hidden. While concealed, I observed people moving up and down the same street. It seemed they were searching for me. Among them was a familiar figure, my brother, walking under the streetlights.

I don't know who had contacted him or how he knew to come, as he lived far from the scene and couldn't have heard the commotion from his home. I watched from the shadows, unsure whether to reveal myself. After some time, once I felt physically and emotionally stable enough, I decided to walk away from the area. After escaping the traumatic incident in Extension 9, I began walking toward the city of Germiston.

As I approached the vicinity of the Enterprise factory, I noticed several vehicles on the road. They were stationary and the presence of multiple cars heightened my anxiety. I was deeply traumatized and did not want to be seen by anyone. In that moment of fear and vulnerability,

I altered my course and made my way to Strachan Hostel in Extension 8. There, I encountered a longtime friend who, noticing my bare chest and lack of shoes, offered me a jacket.

His gesture brought not only physical relief but also a reassuring sense of safety. While we were speaking, a police vehicle passed by. Its presence was a reminder of the seriousness of what had occurred and it added to the surreal nature of the evening. After sharing my experience, I made the decision to return to Extension 9 to understand what had happened and to seek clarity. He volunteered to walk with me back toward Extension 9, accompanying me until we reached the entrance separating Ext 8 from Ext 9.

Sezela street was quiet when I arrived. I went back to the house I had been visiting before the incident, retracing my steps to the place where the events had unfolded. Upon returning to the house I had been visiting prior to the attack, I found only one person present. She had just arrived and was unaware of what had transpired earlier. Using her cellphone, she contacted others to inquire about their whereabouts.

The response came from someone who explained that they were near Enterprise Factory, located on Linton Street in Germiston and that the police were in the process of arresting the vehicle. I asked her to request that they bring along my clothing and work equipment, which had been left inside the car during the incident. Approximately an hour later, they arrived, accompanied by one of the individuals who had been inside the vehicle at the time of the attack.

When I inquired about the car, I was informed that it had been taken to the Germiston Police Station by two officers, with assistance from the same local resident who had intervened earlier, the driver of the ford ranger. Despite my efforts to gather information, none of the individuals present could provide any clarity about what had occurred. Each claimed to have no knowledge of the events leading up to or following the attack. Following the traumatic events in Extension 9, I spent the night in the same room with one of the individuals who had been present during the incident.

When I woke early the next morning, around 05:00, he was still asleep. I decided to leave quietly and head to the Germiston Police Station to report what had happened. However, upon reaching the station gate, I was overwhelmed by physical pain and emotional distress. I hesitated, then turned back.Instead of entering, I made a phone call to someone I trusted and informed him of the events from the previous night.

He was shocked and urged me to meet him at his home. I boarded a minibus taxi to Kathlehong, Siluma View, and arrived about an hour later, leaving the other individual behind in Extension 9. After sharing my story, I was given stark advice: "Surrender yourself or leave the country." Despite the gravity of those words, I was reassured that legal assistance would be arranged through trusted contacts in the legal profession. Later that morning, I received a call from the individual I had left behind.

He asked where I was and eventually joined me in Kathlehong. Once reunited, we discussed the situation and agreed that I should seek medical attention before approaching the police. It was still the morning following the incident. Throughout our conversations, he remained evasive when I asked direct questions, particularly about the child mentioned during the attack. I chose to accept his silence, focusing instead on recovery and next steps.

He and my confidant went to a nearby Spaza shop to buy food, leaving me behind. When I offered to accompany them, they declined. Around 11:00 a.m. on 2nd of November 2018, I went to Ramokonopi Clinic in Kathlehong for medical treatment, accompanied by the same individual who had been with me the night before.

After leaving Ramokonopi Clinic in Katlehong, part of the Ekurhuleni Metropolitan Municipality, we spent the rainy afternoon traveling to Spruit View, where I stayed at a residence for nearly two weeks. During this time, I was accompanied by someone who had been present during the hijacking incident. He had been a passenger in the vehicle and was among those who disappeared with the car during the chaos.

Although we had once shared a friendship, his behavior in the aftermath of the incident raised serious concerns. Whenever I asked direct questions about what had happened, especially about the child mentioned during the attack, he would deflect or avoid answering.

I never heard him say, "Yes, I saw the child." Instead, he would respond vaguely, often repeating phrases like "bayakusukela" (they are chasing you), without offering clarity. His reluctance to engage, his emotional detachment and his refusal to assist in uncovering the truth made me feel unsafe.

I began to see him not as a friend, but as someone who might be monitoring me, someone whose silence spoke louder than words. Though I had no concrete evidence, I felt betrayed. He had not been attacked, despite being in the same car and his evasiveness only deepened my suspicion.

He offered accommodation, but nothing more. No support in seeking justice, no answers to my questions and no acknowledgment of the trauma I had endured. When I raised topics related to the incident, he would either change the subject or physically remove himself from the conversation. If the question was directed at him personally, he would do everything possible to avoid it.

This experience left me feeling isolated and emotionally exposed. The person I had trusted was now a source of uncertainty. His actions, more than his words, suggested that he knew more than he was willing to share. I knew that pressing further for answers from the individual who had been with me during the hijacking would likely escalate into conflict.

His demeanor made it clear, he was not going to cooperate and he seemed prepared for confrontation if pushed. Violence was not a solution, especially in a situation already fraught with fear and uncertainty. Meanwhile, I learned that a woman connected to the local resident who had intervened during the incident had been calling persistently.

She was asking about my whereabouts and questioning why I hadn't handed myself over to the police. She claimed her family was now in trouble because of me. The day after receiving medical treatment, I went to the Germiston Police Station to inquire about the release of my vehicle, it was 3rd November 2018. I was accompanied by the same individual and another trusted person. Upon arrival, we spoke to a staff member who was unfamiliar with the case.

He went to check internally and returned with the name of the officer assigned to investigate. The officer was stationed on the fourth floor of the building. On our way up, we encountered another officer who asked a few preliminary questions and directed us to the correct office. At that point, my confidant remained outside while I entered with the individual who had been shadowing me since the incident. His behavior had become increasingly controlling.

He insisted on accompanying me everywhere, whether to the bathroom, a nearby shop or even during phone calls. I complied, sensing that resistance might provoke further tension. When we met the investigating officer, Warrant officer Coetzee, he was dressed in a striped khaki short-sleeved shirt, khaki trousers and carried a firearm on his waist. I introduced myself and explained the purpose of our visit. I chose not to disclose the full details of the incident, particularly the part involving the child, due to my suspicions about the individual accompanying me.

Warrant officer Coetzee's first question was about the ownership of the vehicle. I confirmed that I was the owner and presented proof. He then informed us that the car had been discovered the previous night by two officers patrolling near Enterprise Factory on Linton Jones Street in Germiston. In possession of the vehicle were three individuals; Sivenkosi Gontsana, Sithembile Sibanda, and Thulani kubayi.

The driver had been unable to continue driving due to mechanical failure, possibly caused by a fuel transmission issue linked to the car's security system not being properly disengaged. During my first meeting with the investigating officer at Germiston Police Station, I was asked whether I knew Thulani Kubayi, the individual identified as the driver of my vehicle at the time it was recovered.

According to the officer, Thulani is a resident of Extension 9 and was one of the three occupants found inside the car near Enterprise Factory on Linton Jones Street. I responded truthfully, I had no knowledge of Thulani Kubayi, nor had I ever given him permission to drive my car. There was no agreement between us, formal or informal. I had never met him before and I could not explain how or why he came to be in possession of my vehicle.

That marked the conclusion of my initial interview with the investigating officer. Although I had hoped for more clarity or direction, the encounter left me with more questions than answers particularly about how my vehicle ended up in the hands of strangers and why those closest to me during the incident remained silent or evasive.

Chapter 04
Detention

By the 3rd of November 2018, three days after the hijacking incident, a criminal case had not yet been registered, and no warrant of arrest had been issued. During my initial interview with the investigating officer at Germiston Police Station, I was instructed to return home and await further communication once the investigation formally commenced.

At that time, I had already vacated my residence in Extension 9 due to the trauma I had experienced. I was temporarily staying at a friend's place, emotionally and physically destabilized. The impact of the incident extended beyond personal safety, my employment was abruptly terminated without any formal communication. My manager's resignation had already been approved, leaving me without support, income or a stable place to stay in the months ahead.

After spending two days in Spruit View, I returned to Germiston. While still in Spruit View, I received a phone call from my brother. He informed me that he and others had begun negotiating with the family who had falsely claimed that my car had struck their child.

According to him, the family had decided not to pursue a criminal case against me. Instead, they were preparing to repatriate the child's body to Zimbabwe. Their request, as relayed to me, was not legal action, but rather financial assistance and a formal apology. This demand was deeply unsettling, given the circumstances and the lack of clarity surrounding the incident.

The emotional toll of being falsely implicated, combined with the loss of employment and housing, left me in a state of profound distress. In the days following the hijacking incident, I received a call from my brother, who informed me of ongoing negotiations with the family that had claimed my vehicle had struck their child. According to him, the family had decided not to pursue a criminal case.

Their reasoning was rooted in cultural beliefs, they stated that this was not the first time they had lost a child in a road accident and suspected that the tragedy was linked to unresolved ancestral or ritual matters within their family. The family, originally from Zimbabwe but residing in South Africa, expressed a strong desire to repatriate the child's body.

Both parents were unemployed and in urgent need of financial assistance. They requested R20,000, or R15,000 if it could be provided immediately, to cover the costs of transporting the body to Zimbabwe.

It's important to note that I did not formally appoint anyone to negotiate on my behalf. The individuals involved, my brother and a local resident, the driver of the ford ranger i mentioned earlier, acted voluntarily and I acknowledged and appreciated their efforts. However, their involvement also introduced pressure and expectations that I had not authorized.

One of the local resident's family members later told my former associate that I needed to "clear their names" by either paying the requested amount or surrendering myself to the police. She claimed that her family was being blamed for not encouraging me to take responsibility. This statement added emotional weight and complexity to an already traumatic situation.

At that point, I was still grappling with the aftermath, physically injured, emotionally destabilized and without employment or stable housing. The pressure to respond to financial demands, cultural interpretations and community expectations compounded my distress. I was navigating a landscape of suspicion, silence and informal negotiations, all while trying to understand what had truly happened and how to protect myself.

The day after the incident, while still in Kathlehong, we made the decision to block a persistent caller someone who had been repeatedly contacting us about the same issue. Her tone and urgency suggested confusion and frustration, as if her expectations or plans had not unfolded as intended.

I interpreted her reaction as one of disappointment, possibly because I had not been arrested immediately after the incident, nor had I shared my account with anyone who had not been present at the scene. That was my reading of her behavior.

My brother, too, appeared dissatisfied with my response regarding financial assistance. The following day, I received a call from another individual involved in the informal negotiations. He relayed that the family wanted a direct apology from me and insisted that I come alone to deliver it. The request was framed as a gesture of closure to allow the grieving family time to mourn and move forward.

An appointment was set and we met at the home of the person facilitating the negotiations. However, during the meeting, the plan for a personal apology was cancelled. Out of concern for my safety, it was decided that the apology would be delivered on my behalf. There were fears that the family, still emotionally raw, might react violently if I appeared in person.

At that meeting, I was presented with two options; Pay R20,000 directly to assist with the repatriation of the child's body to Zimbabwe or Transfer ownership of my vehicle in exchange for the family's financial relief, with the negotiators handling the payment on my behalf. These options were presented not as legal resolutions, but as emotional and cultural gestures intended to bring closure.

Yet for me, they carried the weight of unresolved trauma, suspicion and the loss of control over my own narrative. Although I verbally agreed to contribute financially toward the family's request, I made no firm commitment regarding the timing. The urgency was acknowledged, but I was navigating trauma, instability and uncertainty.

I was given two days to respond, yet a few days later, the individual who had been facilitating the negotiations withdrew from the process, citing my lack of interest in meeting the family halfway. Our final exchange ended with a simple "goodbye" over the phone. The withdrawal was accompanied by accusations, directed not only at me, but also at those who had been close to me during the incident.

They were accused of misleading me, of obstructing resolution. The pressure mounted from multiple directions and trust began to erode. I recall one comment from a close friend of my brother, who speculated that the grieving family might ultimately benefit financially from the tragedy.

He referenced another case where a family's children had died in similar circumstances and afterward, they allegedly became wealthy. It was just a story, but in that moment, I had already lost trust in nearly everyone around me. My brother, too, expressed frustration, not just with me, but with those who had been supporting me. He believed they were leading me astray.

The same sentiment was echoed by the negotiator who had withdrawn, urging me to "solve this challenge alone" and insisting that my friends were misleading me. But I could not take him seriously. His tone, his demands and his conclusions felt unreasonable and disconnected from the emotional and legal complexity of what I was facing. I was being asked to carry the weight of resolution, apology and financial restitution without clarity, without support and without trust.

On 19 November 2018, I was invited to the Germiston Police Station by Warrant officer Coetzee. At the time, I was already in the City of Germiston, from Katlehong South where I was temporarily accommodated by my friend, which allowed me to arrive at the station within minutes of receiving the invitation trough a phone call.

I attended the meeting alone. Notably, the individuals who had previously accompanied me, seemingly with the intent to observe or monitor my reactions, were not present that morning. Their absence marked a significant shift in the tone and privacy of the engagement.

The meeting was convened at Warrant officer Coetzee's request and I understood it to be part of his ongoing investigation into the circumstances surrounding the seizure of my motor vehicle and the events that followed. The environment was markedly more focused and direct, allowing for a clearer exchange of information without external influence or distraction.

As I made my way to the office, I encountered a Lieutenant Colonel who made it clear, in front of the investigating officer, that I was to be arrested that day, He known parents of the child alleged to be killed by my vehicle. Warrant officer Coetzee asked a few questions and informed me that he would be taking my official statement. He claimed to have gathered sufficient information to open a criminal case, insisting that my vehicle had struck a child and that a culpable homicide case would be registered.

He further stated that residents of Extension 9 had confirmed to him that my car was involved in the incident. He added, "Unfortunately, you are not going to get your car back, the state will sell it." He also advised me to open a case of vehicle theft against Thulani Kubayi, the individual found driving my car without permission. However, before I could act on that advice, he proceeded to arrest me.

I reminded him that the alleged incident never occurred. His response was chilling, "The court shall free you, I am going to arrest you anyway." That was the end of the discussion. Warrant officer Coetzee then asked about my home province and remarked, "You come from as far as your province only to disturb people in Johannesburg who are busy with serious business." His words were demeaning and dismissive. I did not respond further. He had already told me the car would be sold, and now he was questioning my presence in the city.

I was demoralized, confused and emotionally overwhelmed. He ordered me to place my hands behind my back, handcuffed me, and escorted me to the police holding cells. Once inside, I called my brother to inform him of my arrest. He arrived about an hour later. I had no solution except to hope for justice. I believed that whatever corruption or crime had occurred, the court of law would separate truth from lies.

Chapter 05

Statement about the arrest

Following my arrest, I explained the full circumstances to my brother, including details of my initial conversation with Warrant officer Coetzee. My brother was visibly shocked. According to him, no member of our family had opened a criminal case related to the incident.

This was later confirmed by Warrant Officer Coetzee during our first meeting, no case had been registered, no statements had been taken from the Ekurhuleni Metropolitan Police Department (EMPD) and in fact, the only information in circulation was what Coetzee had received from the police official who had seized the motor vehicle.

Warrant officer Coetzee informed me that this information had only come to his attention on the morning of 1 November 2018. He indicated that, as part of his investigation, he intended to consult EMPD for formal statements. He had been told by two SAPS officers that on 31 October 2018, an EMPD official had refused to provide a statement.

This refusal, according to Coetzee, was the reason no arrest or further action was taken on 3 November 2018, when I had voluntarily gone to the police station to report the vehicle. Despite this, Warrant officer Coetzee advised me to consider opening a criminal case. However, he emphasized that he first wanted to conduct his own inquiries and hear directly from those alleged to have been present at the scene.

At that point, he was unaware that the EMPD officials had since changed their position. He had recently been in contact with them and believed they were not pursuing any criminal charges. After hearing my account in full, I left the police station hoping that warrant officer Coetzee will resume investigations and release the motor vehicle.

I was left disappointed and disillusioned. The allegations against me were malicious and I could not understand the motive behind this unlawful arrest. Yet I remained committed to seeking justice through lawful means, trusting that the truth would eventually prevail.

On the 3rd of November 2018, I walked into the Germiston police station seeking answers. My vehicle had been seized under circumstances that made no legal or procedural sense. I met with Warrant Officer Coetzee, hoping for clarity.

What I received instead was a troubling admission that there were no formal statement had been made or presented to him by any police officer or witness to justify the seizure. He had nothing in hand, no affidavits, no signed declarations, only hearsay from two constables who had been on duty on the 31st of October.

Despite this glaring absence of evidence, Coetzee advised me to open a criminal case against the individual who had been found in possession of my vehicle. This advice came before any investigation had been conducted, before any consultation with the Ekurhuleni Metropolitan Police Department (EMPD), and before any facts had been verified.

It was a recommendation made in haste, without foundation and without regard for due process. I left that meeting expecting that, at the very least, Coetzee would now begin collecting proper witness affidavits, statements dated after our discussion, reflecting a genuine attempt to investigate the matter.

But when I later reviewed the docket, I was stunned to find that all the statements had been dated before our meeting. Even more perplexing was the sudden appearance of a witness statement dated the 31st of October 2018, the very date Coetzee had previously insisted yielded no formal documentation. This contradiction raised serious questions about the integrity of the record.

The inconsistencies didn't stop there. A statement from the EMPD, which Coetzee had claimed was never taken at the scene, had somehow materialized in the file. This was despite multiple individuals present at the scene including the constable who initiated the seizure, confirming that no such statement had been taken. The narrative was shifting and not in a way that aligned with the truth.

Then came the most disturbing discovery of all, a statement allegedly deposed by me. It was a complete fabrication. The document contained false personal information, incorrect dates and details I had never provided to anyone. It was as if someone had constructed a version of me on paper, one that served a predetermined narrative rather than the truth.

The deception extended to the forensic and postmortem reports. One such report was attributed to a paramedic whose identity could not be verified. The contents of these documents were riddled with contradictions and crucially, they placed me far from the alleged crime scene allegedly took place at Arkin and Linton Jones Street, at the time of the incident.

I had never been to that location on that date, nor had I been involved in any event that could justify the allegations being constructed around me. What became painfully clear was that Warrant Officer Coetzee had failed in his duty to conduct a proper investigation.

He had relied on information so unreliable, so procedurally flawed, that no reasonable officer acting in good faith could have used it to justify an arrest or seizure. The entire process was marred by negligence, fabrication and a disregard for the principles of justice.

As I continued to examine the case file, the inconsistencies deepened. Among the documents were statements attributed to two individuals, one claiming to be an official from the Ekurhuleni Metropolitan Police Department (EMPD), and the other allegedly a paramedic from the Emergency Medical Services (EMS).

Both identities were presented as authoritative sources, their statements used to reinforce the narrative surrounding the seizure of my vehicle and the alleged incident. But when I conducted my own verification, the truth emerged, neither of these individuals was employed by the City of Ekurhuleni.

Their names did not appear on any official personnel registers and their affiliations could not be confirmed through municipal channels. These were not just procedural errors, they were deliberate insertions of false authority into the evidentiary record.

The implications were staggering. Statements from individuals falsely presented as EMPD and EMS officials had been used to justify actions taken against me. Their fabricated authority lent weight to a case built on contradiction and hearsay. It became clear that the investigation had not only failed to meet the minimum standards of due process, but it had also actively misled.

This revelation added another layer to the institutional failure I was confronting. It was no longer just about a mishandled investigation or a negligent officer. It was about systemic misconduct, where false identities and forged documentation were allowed to shape the course of justice. The very institutions meant to protect the public had, in this instance, become instruments of deception.

Chapter 06

Detained without due process

On the morning of 19 November 2018, at approximately 10:55, I was arrested and detained in the holding cells of Germiston Police Station. I remained there overnight until 08:30 on 20 November, when proceedings resumed. From there, I was transferred to the Magistrate Court holding cells, and subsequently to Boksburg Prison, where I remained in custody until 27 November 2018.

On that day, my bail application was finally heard and granted. Despite my release, my motor vehicle remained in custody without any lawful justification under the legislation governing the seizure and disposal of articles. The continued impoundment of my property blatantly undermined constitutional safeguards against arbitrary deprivation, violating my rights under the law.

The matter dragged on for years. It proceeded from 20 November 2018 to 14 June 2021, and again from 17 August 2022 to 6 April 2023. Throughout this prolonged ordeal, due process was repeatedly ignored.

Crucially, the false EMPD and EMS affidavits was submitted by individuals who were not employed by the City of Ekurhuleni, were accepted into the record without authentication. The identity of the fake EMPD official was never verified and no effort was made to confirm the legitimacy of the paramedic's credentials before admission as evidence in the proceedings. This was not merely a procedural oversight, it was a systemic failure.

The acceptance of unauthenticated affidavits, the unlawful seizure of property, and the extended detention without proper investigation all pointed to a justice process that had lost its integrity. I was not just fighting for my freedom, I was fighting for the principle that truth must be verified and rights must be respected. On 14 June 2021, the matter was adjourned without a future date. The reason given was the unavailability of witnesses, yet no explanation was offered to me, the accused.

I was left in legal limbo, prejudiced by a delay that had no justification. My property remained in custody and the case itself hung in suspension. No accountability was demanded of the witnesses who failed to appear. Later, the matter was reinstated without consequence to those who had caused the delay. It raised a question that still echoes, Does the law permit such impunity? And if not, why there were no consequences?

Then, on 6 April 2023, the matter reached its conclusion, with a conviction and sentence handed down against me. But the judgment was not supported by any reliable or substantive evidence. The very witnesses whose statements had been used to justify my arrest had abandoned those statements.

They were allowed to introduce new allegations, claims that were never present at the time of my arrest, never captured in their original affidavits and never subjected to proper scrutiny. Instead of being discharged, I was prosecuted, convicted and sent to prison without lawful justification. The conviction was secured using fraudulent documents, paperwork that should never have been admitted into evidence.

The court accepted unauthenticated affidavits from individuals falsely presented as EMPD and EMS officials, whose identities were never verified. The very foundation of the case was built on deception. As I sat with the weight of the judgment, I began to compare the market value of the property they were attempting to take from me with the value of the justice system they undermined. What is the price of truth?

What is the cost of a conviction built on lies? When court procedures are disregarded, and constitutional protections are trampled, the damage goes far beyond material loss. It strikes at the heart of public trust and it leaves individuals like me fighting not just for property but for dignity, truth and the rule of law. The final blow came not from the evidence, but from the court itself.

On 6 April 2023, the matter was concluded with a conviction and sentence, but the judgment was not based on truth. The judicial process did not correct these violations. It endorsed them. The court accepted fabricated affidavits, unauthenticated identities and procedural shortcuts that undermined the integrity of the trial.

Instead of dismissing the case or demanding accountability, the system chose to prosecute and convict, not on lawful grounds, but on a foundation of deception. This was not justice. It was a betrayal of the very principles the court was meant to uphold. And it left me asking, If the law does not punish fraud within its own walls, what protection remains for the innocent? When a person is wrongfully accused, society rarely waits for the verdict.

Chapter 07

Technicalities in the process

My case was heard at Germiston Magistrate Court, located at 87B President Street. I faced three witnesses and waited for the opportunity to tell my side of the story. My legal team had been ready since early 2019, but the trial was delayed repeatedly due to;

The postmortem report that took over four months to arrive, COVID-19 protocols disrupted court operations, Witnesses failed to appear on multiple occasions, The docket was missing or not brought to court at times, My legal team disappeared without explanation.

Earlier in the proceedings, I had formally requested through my legal defence and directly to the presiding judicial officer that the authenticity of the postmortem report be tested. I believed the document was fraudulent, and that it did not truthfully reflect the circumstances of the alleged death. My request was acknowledged but never ventilated in subsequent appearances. The silence around this critical issue was deafening.

At one point in 2019, following yet another postponement, I sought to verify the next court date. I was informed by the registrar of a date that contradicted the one issued during the proceedings. Acting on that information, I appeared in court on the incorrect date only to be told I had missed the actual scheduled appearance.

When I checked the court's logbook, I discovered the date had been altered. This manipulation occurred during a time of intense emotional strain. I was out on bail, pending finalization of the proceedings and I began to suspect that these errors were not accidental. It felt like a deliberate attempt to secure my re-arrest.

In South African law, failure to appear in court as an accused person amounts to contempt, a punishable offence. That was my conclusion, a conspiracy to entrap me through procedural misdirection.

Despite the chaos, I held onto hope that the truth would eventually surface. But the delays, the inconsistencies and the silence around critical evidence painted a picture of a system struggling or unwilling to deliver justice.

As the legal delays mounted, so did the personal cost. By this time, I was unemployed, with no steady income to support myself or cover the escalating legal fees. I had a responsibility to pay my lawyer, but on many occasions, I simply could not afford to.

When that happened, the case would either be postponed again or I would have to negotiate with my legal team, who, despite their commitment, began to express concern about my deteriorating financial situation.

I had also lost my accommodation of choice. I was no longer able to afford rent and was now relying on the generosity of others, friends and acquaintances who offered me temporary shelter. Eventually, I relocated to a municipal hostel, a place often used by those in crisis or displacement. It was a humbling and painful transition from independence to dependency, from stability to survival.

This period was marked by emotional exhaustion, legal uncertainty and social isolation. Yet I continued to show up in court, to prepare for trial, and to hold onto the belief that the truth would eventually be heard.

Throughout the course of my case, I was repeatedly advised to seek external consultation, to approach legal aid organizations, advocacy groups and independent experts who might assist me. What many did not know was that I had already done so. I had reached out to multiple organizations, some of which were well aware of my case.

I submitted documents, explained my situation, and waited for support that never fully materialized. Some acknowledged the injustice. Others expressed sympathy. But few were willing to intervene. Whether it was fear, bureaucracy or political caution, the result was the same I stood alone.

The most painful betrayal came from within, from the very legal defence I had trusted to protect my rights. Over time, I began to sense that my representation was no longer aligned with my interests. Promises were made and not kept. Critical evidence was ignored. Strategic decisions were taken without my input.

It was not just neglect. It felt like abandonment. That betrayal forced me to consider the unthinkable, representing myself. I began studying legal procedure, reviewing case law and preparing to speak in court without formal counsel. It was not a choice made out of pride, it was a necessity born of survival.

As I navigated the legal terrain, I began to understand the magnitude of what I was facing. This was not just a flawed case, it was a system compromised by deep infiltration, where state officials could act with impunity, and where individuals could be coerced or forced to act against their will.

I saw how documents could be fabricated, how court dates could be manipulated, how silence could be weaponized. I saw how truth could be buried beneath layers of procedure and how justice could be delayed until it no longer resembled justice at all. Studying the law and trying to understand court proceedings was never smooth.

The structure of legal rules, the language of procedure, and the culture of the courtroom were not designed for people like me, individuals forced to navigate justice without institutional support. I encountered resistance not just from the system, but from those around me.

Every time I mentioned self-representation, I was met with discouragement. "You need a lawyer," they said. "You won't make it on your own." That refrain became a chorus, one that annoyed me deeply. Why such certainty in the face of a Constitution that explicitly protects the right to represent oneself?

Why such doubt when the law itself affirms the dignity and agency of the accused? It raised a painful question, Was there any real regard for constitutional dictates or human rights in practice? The answer, I believe, is no. But I will deal with that in my next book.

The saying "justice delayed is justice denied" has become almost cliché in South Africa, repeated in courts, classrooms and conferences. Yet it is only when you live through that delay, when you watch your life dissolve while waiting for justice to move, that you truly understand its meaning.

For years, I sat in courtrooms waiting for progress that never came. Dates were set, then postponed. Witnesses vanished, files disappeared, and each postponement felt like another wound, small, silent, but cumulative. The law that promises "speedy and fair trial" under section 35 of the constitution became an illusion.

In theory, justice is blind. In practice, it often turns its head. Court delays are not merely administrative inconveniences, they are weapons, subtle, procedural instruments that grind the innocent into submission.

Each postponement brought new costs, transport to court, lost opportunities, emotional exhaustion, and the constant anxiety of uncertainty. I watched months turn into years while the system idled, unmoved by the urgency of a life on hold.

I had complied with every rule, every requirement. Yet, compliance seemed to count for nothing when the system itself was indifferent. The same Constitution that guarantees fairness also demands efficiency, but that principle seems to vanish somewhere between the paperwork and the courtroom door.

Justice cannot exist in theory alone. It must live in the rhythm of action, in accountability, in deadlines, in the respect of time. When time itself becomes a tool of punishment, the system has already failed.

Waiting for justice is a kind of imprisonment, invisible but suffocating. For me, those years felt like standing in a corridor between accusation and vindication, never allowed to move forward or go back. Every sunrise brought the same question, Will this ever end?

Every night, the same echo, What if it never does? The delays didn't just affect my case; they invaded every part of my existence. Work opportunities disappeared, Friends withdrew. Even my sense of identity was slowly eroded by uncertainty.

I began to understand that injustice is not only about wrongful conviction, it's also about systemic neglect, the quiet kind that kills dreams instead of bodies. South Africa's justice system is built on strong laws but weakened by poor practice.

Our Constitution is one of the most advanced in the world, yet its implementation often falls victim to politics, inefficiency and corruption. Too often, justice becomes a privilege for the wealthy and a burden for the poor.

Delays affect those without influence the most, people like me, who cannot afford private investigators, powerful representation or political protection. I began to see that my experience was not an exception, it was a reflection of a systemic disease, one that erodes public confidence and deepens social inequality.

Each adjournment, each unanswered letter, each ignored appeal to authority was not just a failure of my case, but a failure of the nation's promise to its people. But from every failure, there are lessons, harsh, but necessary.

Through those years, I learned that real justice is not handed down by courts alone, it is also built by communities, activists, and ordinary people who refuse to be silent. I realized that knowledge is power and that ignorance is the soil in which injustice grows.

The more people understand their rights, how the system should work, what timelines are reasonable, what procedures protect them, the harder it becomes for injustice to hide behind bureaucracy. This realization reshaped my life. It turned my anger into purpose and my wounds into weapons of awareness.

It is why I established the Human Rights Association of South Africa (HRASA) not to complain about what had been done to me, but to make sure others never experience the same. HRASA became my response to the question that haunted me, What happens to the ordinary person who faces a system that forgets them?

Our answer is simple: we empower them. We teach them. We stand with them until justice becomes more than a promise, until it becomes a lived reality. Even now, years later, my case remains a scar, but also a compass. It reminds me that true justice requires more than good laws, it requires good conscience.

It demands a culture where accountability is not optional and where public institutions serve with integrity, not fear or favour. The justice I believe in is not one that punishes blindly, but one that restores, redeems and rebuilds.

That belief keeps me going, even when the path remains lonely and steep. The system may have delayed my justice, but it did not defeat it. Instead, it awakened in me a vision larger than my own pain, a mission to transform isolation into empowerment and injustice into education.

"They thought by delaying my case they could delay my destiny. But justice, though late, walks with those who refuse to stop." Justice delayed is not the end. It is a call, a demand that someone, somewhere, must rise and make it right. For me, that calling became HRASA. And through it, I have learned that while courts may move slowly, truth, once awakened, never sleeps again.

Chapter 08

Irregularities and property rights

As the years of court proceedings dragged on, I began to see l that could not be dismissed as coincidence. What had begun as a single criminal case slowly revealed the fingerprints of a coordinated network of individuals, masquerading as witnesses but behaving more like members of an organized syndicate.

Their actions were not driven by justice, but by manipulation, deliberate efforts to frustrate due process and destroy my credibility. Their strategy was simple yet calculated, they wanted me to miss a court appearance. If I failed to appear, a warrant for my arrest would automatically be issued, branding me as "absconding" and ensuring my immediate re-detention.

It was a cruel psychological trap, one that depended on my exhaustion, poverty, and despair. But they underestimated me. Despite every obstacle, every humiliation, and the enormous emotional and financial toll, I attended every hearing.

Each time my name was called, I stood up. I refused to let lies write the final chapter of my story. Ironically, it was not I who failed the process, it was the system and its own witnesses. Their repeated non-attendance stalled the proceedings again and again. By June 2021, the court had already declared the matter trial-ready, yet the trial could not proceed.

On 14 June 2021, the case was adjourned indefinitely, with no future date set. Justice, in effect, was suspended, not by my conduct, but by administrative neglect and procedural irregularity. Amid all this, another injustice quietly grew, one that symbolized everything wrong with the process, the unlawful detention of my vehicle. On 31 October 2018, my car was seized following the incident.

On 3 November 2018, I personally reported it as stolen, believing the system would protect my rights as a lawful owner. Instead, on 19 November 2018, I was arrested and proceedings began the very next day, on the 20th. Years passed. The matter stalled. The case was adjourned without conclusion. Yet through all this time, from 2018 to 2021 and beyond, my car remained in police custody, untouched, unreleased and unaccounted for.

This was not merely an administrative oversight. It was a direct violation of Sections 20 to 31 of the Criminal Procedure Act 51 of 1977, which clearly outline how law enforcement may seize, hold, and dispose of property. The law is explicit, Property may be retained only if it is required for evidentiary purposes or if there is a valid forfeiture order issued by a competent court.

If neither condition exists, the property must be returned to its lawful owner without delay. None of these conditions were satisfied in my case. No forfeiture order was ever issued. No ongoing evidentiary need was proven. The indefinite adjournment should have automatically triggered the release of my property. Instead, it remained impounded, a silent hostage of procedural negligence. That vehicle became more than just a possession, it became a symbol of the state's disregard for individual rights.

Each day it sat in custody, it reminded me that in South Africa, the very systems meant to protect the innocent can sometimes become the instruments of deprivation. Through all this, I remained steadfast in my compliance with the law. Over a span of twenty-five months, I appeared in court more than fourteen times. Each trip carried financial costs I could scarcely afford, transport fares, legal consultations, lost time, all while unemployed and surviving through the goodwill of others.

I respected every order, every instruction, every condition of my bail. I kept faith in the system, even as it repeatedly failed me. Yet the state, in return, did not uphold its side of the social contract. Justice delayed became justice denied. Property unlawfully withheld became a breach of constitutional rights particularly Section 25 of the Constitution, which protects against arbitrary deprivation of property.

A System that breaks Its own rules. The Criminal Procedure Act is not optional. It was written to ensure fairness, transparency, and accountability in criminal proceedings. When the state itself violates those provisions, when it withholds property without authority, when it allows cases to stagnate without cause, it sends a chilling message, that law is a tool for the powerful, not a shield for the innocent.

For me, this experience was not just about a car. It was about the principle that every citizen guilty or innocent, has the right to fair treatment, timely justice and lawful process. To lose those rights is to lose faith in the very foundation of democracy.

The irregularities in my case were not isolated incidents, they were symptoms of a broader institutional decay. A car unlawfully detained, witnesses who never appear, cases adjourned indefinitely, all these point to a justice system struggling under the weight of its own contradictions.

And yet, despite everything, I continue to believe in the rule of law, not because it has protected me, but because it must. It is the only framework that can hold both power and people accountable. It is the only hope for those whose rights have been trampled in silence. "When property is taken without cause, it is not only metal and wheels that are lost, it is dignity, faith and the belief that justice still lives.

Chapter 09

Becoming whole again

When a person's world collapses, it rarely happens all at once. It begins quietly in disbelief, in unanswered calls, in the silence that follows when those who once called you friend no longer do. I learned this truth in the years after my arrest and conviction.

The world I once knew of professional respect, independence and trust, vanished overnight. What replaced it was suspicion, fear and isolation. People no longer saw me; they saw a distorted image, shaped by rumours and a system that had failed to seek the truth. Before 31 October 2018, I knew who I was, a financial advisor, respected, reliable and confident in my path.

I was an entrepreneur with vision, a man building toward a secure and meaningful future. But injustice does not only take away your freedom, it tries to steal your identity. Suddenly, every introduction became an explanation, every glance a silent judgment. I was forced to defend not just my innocence, but my existence. The greatest loss was not financial, it was the loss of belonging.

You begin to question yourself, not because you doubt your truth, but because you wonder whether truth still matters in a world that believes lies more easily than facts. It's in that space, between disbelief and despair, that identity begins to crumble. Isolation became both punishment and teacher.

Friends withdrew. Family avoided difficult conversations. Even those who believed in me feared to be seen beside me. The whispers of stigma followed me everywhere, into meetings, into public spaces and into my thoughts. At first, I fought to be heard. But soon, I learned that no amount of explanation could convince those who had already chosen disbelief.

So I turned inward. Silence became my refuge and in that silence, I began to rediscover the fragments of myself that the system and society had tried to erase. The process was painful. There were nights of anger, mornings of emptiness, and long days of reflection filled with one question: Why me?

But slowly I learned that the answer was not in asking why, but in deciding what next. Healing, I discovered, is not about forgetting, it's about transforming pain into power. It is the art of using what broke you to build something stronger.

Freedom came in August 2023, but it did not feel like freedom. The gates of Boksburg correctional centre opened, yet the world outside had changed, or perhaps it was I who had changed beyond recognition. What awaited me was not celebration or closure, but silence.

I stepped out with no job, no car, no stability and no one willing to come close. It was the kind of isolation that cannot be seen, only felt: an invisible wall built from fear and misunderstanding. Upon release, my first act was to seek justice through appeal to claim the fairness the law promised but had denied me. My application for leave to appeal was refused, followed by a petition rejected due to inconsistent transcripts of my trial.

How can truth be weighed when even the record of it is flawed? When I requested the release of my vehicle from SAP13, I was told the investigating officer was unavailable. Later, I was informed that, the car had been destroyed allegedly due to lack of storage space. That single word, destroyed, echoed through me.

It was not just about property. It was about memory, dignity, and evidence, as though erasing the car would erase my story too. Freedom became a different kind of confinement, avoided me. Officials were polite but distant. Even those who once embraced me now spoke in whispers, their eyes carrying the unspoken question, "What if it's true?"

The weight of that doubt was heavier than prison bars. It followed me into every space, every attempt to rebuild. For all its constitutional ideals, South Africa remains a society where accusation too easily overshadows innocence, where people fear association with the accused, even after the truth begins to surface.

I came to understand that stigma is not merely social rejection, it is emotional exile. It separates you from the world. There were nights I could not sleep, haunted by all I had lost, my career, my independence and my sense of belonging. Yet, even in those moments, I refused to surrender to bitterness.

I had already seen how hatred could twist justice and corrode humanity. If I was to heal, I had to choose a different path. Forgiveness became my rebellion not because those who wronged me deserved it, but because I deserved peace. In a world that had reduced me to a false story, I reclaimed my power by writing my own. Perhaps the hardest battle was forgiving myself, not for a crime I never committed, but for ever believing I was less because of it.

I had to remind myself that I was not what had happened to me. I was what I chose to become afterward. It is speaking your truth even when no one listens, and walking with dignity even when the world doubts you.

I am still rebuilding piece by piece, day by day. True recovery is not about restoring what was lost; it is about discovering what cannot be taken. From stigma, I found strength. From isolation, I found identity. And from injustice, I found my calling. Becoming whole again is not about erasing the past, it is about owning it, learning from it, and transforming it into the foundation of purpose.

That is the man I am today: wiser, stronger, and more compassionate. Every scar reminds me not of defeat, but of endurance. Every silence taught me to listen deeper to the voice that still believes in justice, in humanity, and in hope.

Chapter 10

From pain to purpose

There are moments in life when pain demands a purpose. For me, that moment came not in celebration of freedom, but in the silence that followed it. After the gates of Boksburg Correctional Centre closed behind me, I stood in a world that no longer felt familiar.

My name carried a shadow, my career was gone, and my community looked at me with uncertain eyes. Yet beneath that silence, a voice inside me whispered, "Your story is not over, it is the beginning of something greater." That whisper became the seed of a movement within myself, not born from privilege, but from pain; not from theory, but from lived experience.

The vision to dedicate my life to justice and awareness did not emerge overnight. It was shaped by years of reflection, not only on my own experience but on the countless others I had witnessed along the way. In detention, I met men who were not only broken by their sentences but by the system's indifference. Outside, I saw communities trapped in cycles of poverty, ignorance, and fear of authority.

I realized that the greatest prison is not made of walls or bars it is built from silence and lack of awareness. If society was to change, people needed to understand their rights not as distant words written in law books, but as living principles that protect human dignity.

I began speaking to small groups, sharing lessons about rights, fairness, and the law not as a teacher above others, but as someone who had walked through the fire and survived to tell the story. The first steps were small community gatherings, informal talks, and one-on-one conversations with people who had lost hope in the system.

Sometimes, I spoke to crowded rooms. Other times, only two or three people showed up. But I never stopped. Every person reached was a victory against silence. Many came expecting food or relief. Some left disappointed, but a few stayed and listened. That was enough to keep me going.

It became clear that human rights education cannot exist apart from human needs. Knowledge without compassion is powerless. Empowerment begins when people are both informed and supported when dignity is restored alongside awareness. With no funding, no structure, and very little support, I learned to build from nothing but conviction.

Each conversation, each shared truth, each moment of courage, became a stone in the foundation of my renewed life's mission. Helping others understand their constitutional and human rights. Encouraging self-reliance, confidence and inclusion. Standing against injustice through lawful, peaceful means.

I reached out to community leaders and government departments, often without response. But even rejection had meaning, it taught resilience. Every unopened door reminded me that change must often be built from the outside in.

My efforts became a form of healing. Each time I shared what I had endured, I reclaimed a part of what was taken from me. The journey was not about revenge or recognition. It was about reclaiming truth and transforming suffering into something that could serve others. In helping others, I found peace. In speaking truth, I rediscovered my voice.

I came to understand that leadership is not about status or title it is about being present where pain exists, and bringing light where silence reigns. The journey ahead is still long. South Africa continues to wrestle with inequality, corruption, and the erosion of trust. But I believe that even the smallest act of awareness one conversation, one lesson, one moment of courage chips away at those walls.

My dream is to help build a society of conscious citizens, people who think critically, act with integrity, and stand for justice even when it's unpopular. This work this mission is not the end of my story. It is the continuation of it. A living testimony that from injustice, hope can still be born. And from pain, purpose can still rise "They took my freedom, but not my faith. They silenced me, but could not mute my purpose. Today, that purpose has a voice and it will not be silenced again."

Chapter 11
The unfinished struggle

Freedom, they say, begins the moment a man walks out of a cell. But I learned that true freedom begins only when truth is finally heard and that battle, for me, is far from over. After my release from Boksburg correctional centre in August 2023, I carried with me not only the weight of lost years, but also the unfinished pursuit of justice.

My case was more than a legal dispute, it was a test of the very systems meant to protect citizens from abuse of power. And in that test, the system failed. I sought to challenge my unlawful arrest, detention, conviction and sentence, not merely for myself, but as a matter of principle.

I had been arrested on false allegations, detained without lawful justification and convicted in a process riddled with procedural and constitutional irregularities. Yet, when I turned to the same courts for redress, I was met not with fairness, but with obstruction. When I applied for leave to appeal, it was refused.

When I filed a petition, it too was denied not on merit, but because the trial transcripts were incomplete and inconsistent, a failure entirely outside my control. How can justice prevail where the record of truth is missing or altered? How can an innocent man defend himself when the state cannot even preserve the evidence of his trial?

Still, I persisted. I turned to rule 53 of the uniform rules of court, the legal pathway to review administrative action and to hold the system accountable for its decisions. Yet, even there, the doors of justice were shut. When I sought to file my application, I got notification that, I could not be issued a case number because I was "not an attorney of record." It was an insult not just to me, but to the very principle of access to justice guaranteed by our Constitution.

I challenged that decision to a higher court, determined to prove that justice cannot belong only to those with titles or representation. But before my matter could reach the judge's desk, it was intercepted, buried quietly within the machinery of silence that has protected wrongdoing for too long.

That was not just bureaucracy, it was the deliberate denial of a citizen's right to be heard. Most doors I knocked on, from institutions of oversight to those mandated to uphold human rights remained closed.

The Human Rights Commission, oversight bodies and even certain legal aid structures, all turned a blind eye. My case was known, spoken of in whispers, but never confronted openly. Fear, politics and convenience became stronger than conscience.

And yet, I refused to disappear. Through all these setbacks, one truth became clear that the struggle for justice is not fought only in courtrooms, it is fought in persistence, in the will to keep standing even when the law itself bends under the weight of corruption and fear.

The denial of transcripts, the suppression of evidence, the obstruction of access to these are not mere administrative failures. They are human rights violations, each one cutting into the soul of justice itself. What I have faced is not unique to me. It reflects a pattern that many in our country endure, the quiet systematic erosion of rights by those who manipulate the law instead of upholding it.

Each workshop I hold, each young person we teach about their rights, is an act of defiance against the silence that once sought to bury me. Every pamphlet distributed, every public conversation, every community meeting is a reminder that human dignity cannot be destroyed by legal failure.

Looking back, I see the pain, the loss, the betrayal. But I also see growth, the kind that only suffering can teach. They took my car. They took my freedom. They tried to take my name. But they could not take my truth.

That truth has now become my testimony, my advocacy and my mission. The scars remain reminders of the price of justice but they also mark survival, resilience and rebirth. "When justice is denied, humanity itself is on trial."

I still await justice, but I am no longer waiting in silence. My voice, through my story, through this book, is now my evidence. The fight continues not with bitterness, but with clarity. For every person wrongfully accused, for every citizen silenced by fear, for every truth buried beneath procedure, there is hope, there is purpose, and there is power in persistence.

I remain unbroken. The system failed me but it did not define me. It merely revealed the purpose I was born to fulfill: to reform it. Every journey leaves traces, some visible, others etched deep within the soul.

Mine began in a moment of violence and betrayal, travelled through the corridors of injustice, and arrived in a place I never expected: purpose. I often reflect on how a single night in October 2018 changed everything. What began as an act of compassion, stopping to help, became the gateway to years of suffering, loss and public humiliation. But today, I see that same night differently. It was not the end of my story, it was the beginning of my awakening.

Through pain, I discovered purpose. Through isolation, I learned the meaning of faith. And through injustice, I found the calling to defend human dignity, not only my own, but that of others whose voices are silenced by fear, ignorance, or systemic neglect.

My mission is not about one man's fight; it is about building a culture of rights, consciousness, where every person understands their worth and power under the law. Our programs may not yet reach every community, our halls may not yet be full, but every mind we awaken and every injustice we expose is a victory. We speak not from privilege, but from truth, a truth learned in pain, refined in solitude and expressed through service.

To the youth, I say, never surrender your belief in justice. To the poor, the silenced, and the marginalized, your dignity is not negotiable. To those in power, justice delayed is justice denied and history remembers. My fight for legal recognition, for the restoration of my name and for the truth of my case continues.

But I no longer fight as a victim, I fight as a reformer, a survivor and a servant of justice. I carry no hatred, no bitterness. Only conviction. I have seen what injustice can destroy, families, reputations, dreams. But I have also seen what resilience can build, movements, communities and legacies.

I still believe in South Africa. I still believe in our Constitution. What I reject is the silence of those who should protect it. My vision is simple yet profound, a South Africa where no one is silenced, where truth is not a privilege and where justice is not a luxury reserved for the connected or the wealthy.

I dream of a nation that protects its citizens not through fear, but through fairness, where the poor can walk into a courtroom with the same confidence as the powerful. This book is dedicated to that vision, to a rebirth of integrity, accountability and compassion in our justice system and our society. "They may have taken years from my life, but I have taken meaning from those years. And meaning lasts longer than injustice ".

Closing reflection

I walk forward now, not as a man seeking revenge, but as one seeking reform. Not driven by anger, but guided by conviction that justice must serve truth, not power. I no longer walk alone. With me are the countless unseen faces who have endured what I endured: the wrongfully accused, the silenced, the forgotten, the ones who lost everything but still wake each morning believing that life must mean more than survival.

I walk with them and for them. I walk not in shame, but in purpose, because my pain has found its voice and that voice has become a movement of conscience. My wounds no longer represent defeat, they have become lessons written in scars, each one a reminder that injustice cannot define the human spirit.

This is not the end of my story. It is the beginning of ours, the story of a people reclaiming their dignity, their rights, and their power to speak truth, even when the world refuses to listen. Our journey is not about vengeance, but about vision, the vision of a society where no one is silenced for telling the truth, where power answers to principle and where every person, regardless of their past, can stand with dignity before the law.

To those who still walk in the shadows of stigma and fear, know this, you are not alone. The world may doubt you, institutions may fail you, but truth, though delayed, is never destroyed.

Let this story remind us that resilience is greater than rejection, and that hope even when whispered, is louder than silence. I walk forward, carrying no bitterness, only belief, belief that justice can still be restored, that humanity can still be healed, and that purpose born from pain can still change the world.

Afterword

The struggle for justice did not end with my release, it began there. What I endured revealed not only the cracks in our legal system but also the silence of those entrusted to protect the voiceless. Out of that silence was born a conviction that no one should ever walk this path alone again.

Every story like mine is a reminder that human rights are not privileges, they are birthrights. Yet, they mean nothing without courageous people to defend them. I invite every reader to reflect, to question and to act. Whether by speaking out, helping another, or standing up against abuse each act of courage contributes to a larger justice.

The world changes not only through laws, but through hearts that refuse to accept injustice as normal. My hope is that this book ignites such hearts and helps awaken a collective responsibility to protect one another, to expose wrongdoing and to build a society where truth is not feared, but celebrated.

Dedication

To every man and woman who has been silenced, shamed, or forgotten, to those whose cries for justice were met with indifference and to those who still wait for truth to be heard.

May this story remind you that darkness is not the end, it is the place where courage is born.

To the innocent who suffer, the broken who rebuild and the dreamers who still believe that justice can live again, this is for you.

—

Don't miss out!

Visit the website below and you can sign up to receive emails whenever Jubase sakhumzi publishes a new book. There's no charge and no obligation.

https://books2read.com/r/B-A-EAMFC-AMZOE

BOOKS 2 READ

Connecting independent readers to independent writers.

About the Author

Sakhumzi Jubase is a passionate human rights advocate and justice reform activist from South Africa. Deeply moved by the indignity and systemic injustices faced by ordinary people, he has dedicated his life to promoting access to justice and working with institutions to get things right.

Although he has no formal work experience within the justice system, his perspective is shaped by personal encounters, including moments when his own rights were forcefully hijacked. These experiences have driven his commitment to exposing the realities of organized crime, corruption, and abuse of power that undermine justice and human dignity.

How to Defeat Justice reflects both his lived experiences and his unwavering determination to ensure that fairness, accountability,. and respect for human rights prevail.

About the Publisher

how to defeat justice is a true reflection of organised crime syndicate.

Read more at https://sakhumzijubase.co.za.

www.ingramcontent.com/pod-product-compliance
Lightning Source LLC
LaVergne TN
LVHW090430210926
848480LV00002B/769
* 9 7 9 8 2 3 1 5 7 9 2 4 2 *